THE POINTERS SISTERS YOU NEVER KNEW

WHAT YOU SHOULD KNOW ABOUT THE POINTERS SISTERS

NELLY BRIMS

THE POINTER SISTERS YOU NEVER KNEW

What you should know about the pointer Sisters.

By Nelly Brims

certain other non business utilizes allowed by copyright.
2022.

Table of contents

INTRODUCTION

Biography of the pointers sisters.

The Pointer Sisters are a varied and flexible pop/R&B bunch who hail from Oakland, California. The four unique individuals were June, Anita, Ruth and Bonnie Pointer. The women are the little girls of Reverend Elton Pointer and his significant other Sarah and the sisters of siblings Fritz and Aaron. They started their music professions singing in their dad's congregation. Bonnie and June shaped a couple called Pointers, A Couple. Anita before long joined the gathering and the couple turned into a threesome. They began visiting and proceeding as well as providing backing vocals for such specialists as Boz Scaggs, Beauty Smooth, Sylvestor James, and Elvin Diocesan. Ruth joined the gathering in late 1972 and the triplet developed into a group of four. The Pointer Sisters delivered their self-named debut collection in 1973; a funk front of "Yes We Can" crested at #11 on the pop outlines. The subsequent collections ``That is By the drove '' and "Steppin '" similarly got along nicely. "That is By the drove" sire the hit bluegrass tune "Fantasy," which arrived at #13 on the pop charts and won a Grammy Grant for Best Country Execution by a Team or Gathering with Vocal in 1975. The tune "How

Long (Betcha Got a Chick as an afterthought)" from the collection "Steppin'" was a #1 R&B radio hit in 1975. Bonnie left the gathering in 1977 and the band in this way turned into a triplet. In 1978 the Pointer Sisters scored an enormous hit with their hot front of Bruce Springsteen's "Fire," which took off to #2 on the pop diagrams. The Pointer Sisters partook in a consistent progression of dynamic and mixing hit tunes all through the 80s: "He's So Timid," "Slow Hand," "I'm So Energized," "Programmed," "Bounce (for My Adoration)," "Neutron Dance," and "Dare Me." In 1985 "Hop (for My Affection)" won a Grammy Grant for Best Pop Execution by a Team or Gathering with Vocal and "Programmed" won a Grammy Grant for Best Vocal Game plan for At least two Voices. The gathering got a star on the Hollywood Stroll of Popularity in September, 1994 and were drafted into the Vocal Gathering Lobby of Notoriety in 2005. The Pointer Sisters appeared alongside Richard Pryor in the clever satire "Carwash" and facilitated their own television extraordinary "The Pointer Sisters: Up All Nite" in 1987. Among the movies that highlight melodies by the Pointer Sisters on the soundtrack are "Summer Sweethearts," "Night Shift," "Public Parody's Excursion," "Beverly Slopes Cop," "Great," "Offspring of a Lesser God," "Jumpin' Jack Streak," "Stakeout," "Activity Jackson," "Working Young lady," "American Heart," "Donnie Brasco," "Large Mother's Home," "Ali," "Housekeeper in Manhattan," and "Love Really." June Pointer tragically passed on from malignant growth at age 52 on April 11, 2006. The Pointer Sisters keep on acting in shows from one side of

the planet to the other; the ongoing musicians are Ruth
and Anita alongside Ruth's girl Issa.

Chapter one

Anita Pointer

Anita Pointer, one of the four kin vocalists who procured pop accomplishment as The Pointer Sisters, passed on Saturday at 74 years old, her marketing expert reported. She passed on while engaging in malignant growth. Anita was seeing relatives at the hour of her demise, marketing expert Roger Neal said in an explanation. Anita, Ruth, Bonnie and June Pointer, conceived as the little girls of a minister, grew up singing in their dad's congregation in Oakland, California.

Anita Pointer, one of the Grammy-winning Pointer Sisters, had a few pop, country, and R&B melodies during the 1970s and 1980s, including "I'm So Energized," "Hop (For My Adoration)," and "Fire." As per marketing expert Roger Neal, Pointer died at home in Beverly Slopes while encompassed by her loved ones. Anita was the second oldest of four sisters. She joined the gathering as a triplet in the wake of stopping her work as a secretary, June and Bonnie, a couple, in 1969.

Once more the Pointer Sisters later turned into a group of four for some time with Ruth, the only one of the first singing sisters still alive, however Bonnie left the gathering in the last part of the 1970s and they turned into a threesome. Bonnie Pointer left the gathering in

1977, marking a performance to manage Motown
Records yet getting a charge out of just humble
achievement. "We were crushed," Anita Pointer said of
the takeoff in 1990. "We did a show the night she left,
yet from that point forward, we recently halted. We
thought it wouldn't work without Bonnie."

The Pointer Sisters then, at that point, returned to being
a threesome after Bonnie quit the gathering in the last
part of the 1970s. Afterward, Ruth, the last enduring
unique vocal sister, joined the gathering as a group of
four. In 1977, Bonnie Pointer split away from the
threesome and started a performance vocation with
Motown Records, in spite of the fact that she had just a
minor achievement. Anita Pointer commented on the
takeoff in 1990, "We did a show the night she left, yet
from that point forward, we recently halted. We thought it
wouldn't work without Bonnie." Besides, at 52 years old,
June Pointer died from malignant growth in 2006. The
Pointer sisters additionally have two enduring siblings,
Fritz and Aaron.

Before Roxie McKain Pointer, Anita had a little girl
named Jada who died in 2003, passing on Anita to
really focus on Roxie. "While we are profoundly
disheartened by the deficiency of Anita, we are consoled
in realizing she is presently with her girl Jada and her
sisters June and Bonnie and settled. She was the one
that kept us all nearby and together for such a long time.
Her affection for our family will live on in every one of
us," the family said in an explanation.

Their presentation collection in 1973 delivered their most memorable hit single 'Yes We Can'. Among their greatest hits were 'Fire' in 1978, 'He's So Timid' in 1980, 'Slow Hand' in 1981, and 'Neutron Dance', 'Programmed' and 'Hop' in 1983. 'I'm So Energized' from 1982 remains the norm. As of late, the gathering kept performing with Ruth chiming in with her girl Issa and granddaughter Sadako.

HOW SHE PASSED AWAY

Despite the group's increasing fame, it was still an era
long before MTV, and many Nashvillers still hadn't
actually seen the group. As the sisters have recalled in
countless interviews, the Opry show didn't go off without
at least one hitch: "We got onstage to sing the song, and
a guy from the audience stood up and said, 'Well, hot
damn, the girls is black!' " Anita laughs. And despite
being the toast of the town, that lack of visibility caused
other problems in Opryland as well--ones not surprising
to four young black women exploring uncharted terrain.
"When we first performed at the Grand Ole Opry, the
audiences loved us," Anita recalls. "But at the hotel
where there was a party for us, the staff assumed we
were the hired help and directed us toward the back
door."

Undeterred, the Pointers kept charging on--in late '74,
they became the first pop act to perform at the San
Francisco Opera House; tape recorders were running
during the legendary performance, and Live at the
Opera House was released that fall. In 1975, "Fairytale"
won the sisters their first Grammy award, for Best
Country Performance by a Duo or Group (Anita and
Bonnie were also nominated for songwriters of the
year); later, The King himself, Elvis Presley, covered the
tune. That year, the Pointers released their fourth album
for Blue Thumb. Entitled Steppin', the record included
"How Long (Betcha Got A Chick On The Side)";
co-written by Anita and Bonnie, it went Top 20 on the

pop charts and sailed all the way to #1 on R&B. "Going Down Slowly" also scored well on the R&B charts. But soon, it became clear that mere vinyl wasn't enough to contain the Pointer Sisters, and in 1976, the group hit the big screen, joining Richard Pryor in the film, Car Wash. "You Gotta Believe," which was featured on the film's soundtrack, rose up the R&B charts. During this time the Pointers made appearances on the popular children's television show, Sesame Street. Their performances of "Hush Little Baby", "The Alphabet Song" and especially "Pinball Number Count" were replayed often. "Pinball Number Count" became extremely popular and is a fond childhood memory for a generation of viewers.

But despite such upward movement, trouble was brewing in the Pointer household. By 1976, June had dropped out of several performances due to reported health problems, and Bonnie was contemplating a solo career. In 1977, the Pointers released Having A Party, their last album for Blue Thumb. That year, much to her sisters' dismay, Bonnie left the group and signed with Motown Records. "We were devastated," Anita recalled in a 1990 interview. "We did a show the night she left, but after that, we just stopped. We thought it wasn't going to work without Bonnie." Reeling from their sister's departure, the Pointers cut back their touring schedule and contemplated the future. Both Anita and June mulled solo albums (Anita actually recorded one for ABC Records, but it never saw the light of day), while Ruth gave birth to her third child. But eventually, the stage called again, and the Pointer Sisters regrouped as a threesome.

Starting virtually from scratch, the Pointers faced an imposing question: what now? One answer was obvious: they'd thrown away their nostalgic image, because, despite their achievements, the sisters had begun to feel stifled by their earlier success as a jazz act--and the image that they say David Rubinson pushed to continue. "The nostalgia thing got to be artistically frustrating after a while," Anita told Rolling Stone magazine in April 1979. "In the beginning, thrift-store clothes were all we could afford, but then the clothes began dictating the style of music. David saw it as a gimmick we should use, but a lot of the time, I felt really weird. It's hard to be sincere with a pile of fruit on your head."

In an effort to change their style, the sisters signed with Planet Records and teamed up with Richard Perry, a well-known producer who had previously worked with such artists as Barbara Streisand and Carly Simon. Together, they decided to obliterate the past and record a rock 'n roll album. "When Bonnie left the group, we decided we wanted a new direction so people wouldn't miss her, so we got new clothes, a new look, new music, new record producer, new everything," Anita told a reporter in 1986. The change worked: the group's debut single, Bruce Springsteen's "Fire," went all the way to #2 on the pop charts and went gold. Surprisingly, the Sisters say that it's their one hit song that they thought would never make it to the top. "We didn't even know who Bruce Springsteen was at the time," Ruth recalled in a 1997 interview. And Anita was especially hesitant about releasing "Fire" as a single. "I didn't even expect to sing lead on it," she said years later. "It sounded like a low, Ruth-type song to me. We certainly didn't expect it to become a hit." But happily, the sisters were wrong. Boosted by "Fire," the Energy album was certified gold and went on to spawn another top single with "Happiness."

A year later, the Pointers released Priority, which consisted entirely of cover songs by high-profile rock acts. It didn't garner as much attention as its predecessor, but it again proved that the Pointer Sisters could master any musical style--and harmonize like no one else, as evidenced by standouts such as "Dreaming As One." In 1980, the group released their third Planet album, the gold-certified Special Things; it featured the song "Where Did The Time Go," dedicated to their father, Elton, who had passed away in 1979. Anita wrote the title cut and also co-penned "Could I Be Dreaming," which made it to the pop charts, but it was "He's So Shy" that became the album's biggest hit by climbing to #3 and mining gold. In 1981, the group hit it big again with Black & White, which included one of the biggest hits of the year, the Anita-led "Slow Hand." The single topped out at #2 on the Billboard charts, and its instructional lyrics geared toward men who "come and go in a heated rush" became an anthem for women across the country. Next up, "Should I Do It" climbed to #13, and the Black & White album was certified gold. In 1982, the group released So Excited; its first single, "American Music," hit #16, while the follow-up, "I'm So Excited," reached #30.

Early in 1983, June made a move on her own: she released her first solo album, entitled Baby Sister, on Planet Records. The record's first single, "Ready for Some Action," garnered some play on R&B radio, but more importantly, the record's funkier tracks perhaps laid ground for the sisters' next album as a group. Alas, the title of that record summed up exactly what the trio was about to do: Break Out. Upon its release, Stereo Review called the new album "the Pointer Sisters at their sassiest, brassiest, uptempo best." Its first single was "I Need You," a smooth R&B ballad that boasted the tender harmonies of all three sisters--but when Ruth took the lead for "Automatic," her deeper-than-deep vocals practically leapt off the vinyl, and helped the single go all the way to #5.

By now, the video music era had arrived, and with the clip for Break Out's third single, "Jump (for my Love)," the Pointer Sisters landed all over MTV, becoming one of the first black acts to be played in heavy rotation. Boosted by June's energetic vocal, "Jump" raced to #3 on the pop charts. When it came time to release a fourth single, record company executives, who were never happy with "I'm So Excited" chart performance, decided to resurrect the track and give it another shot at the top.

In its resuscitated life, the single finally hit the Top 10 and became a Pointer classic; it was added to the Break Out album over a year into its shelf life. Soon, Paramount Pictures came knocking on the doors of Planet Records, asking for permission to include Break Out's "Neutron Dance" in their upcoming film, Beverly Hills Cop, starring Eddie Murphy. Planet and the Pointer Sisters agreed, and "Neutron Dance," featuring Ruth's gospel-spiked shouts, rose to #6 on the pop charts as its video dominated MTV. Finally, Break Out spawned a sixth single, "Baby Come And Get It," powered by June's sexually charged, raucous vocal. The success of the album earned the sisters two Grammy Awards (Best Vocal by a Duo or Group for "Jump" and Best Vocal Arrangement for "Automatic") and two American Music Awards. Eventually, Break Out was certified triple-platinum, making it the biggest selling album of the Pointer Sisters' career.

While Anita, Ruth and June toured heavily and made countless television appearances,the group made a move to RCA Records, which released the Contact album in 1985. The set's first single, "Dare Me," hit #11 and was accompanied by another stylish video that established the Pointers as trendsetters for a whole new generation. Within three weeks of its release, Contact was certified platinum, and the group went on to win another American Music Award for Best Video Group.

In late 1986, the Pointers released their second album on RCA, Hot Together, which spawned a top 40 hit with

"Goldmine." The Pointers helped promote the album in January '87 by hitting prime time with their first television network special, "Up All Night," featuring Ruth, Anita and June touring Los Angeles night spots with guest stars Whoopi Goldberg, Bruce Willis and The McGuire Sisters. Later that year, the Pointers went back to Beverly Hills with Eddie Murphy; this time, they contributed "Be There" to the soundtrack to Beverly Hills Cop II. The single hit the upper half of Billboard's pop chart and helped the soundtrack album attain multi-platinum status.

In 1987, Anita became the second sister to release a solo album: ``Love For What It Is" was preceded by the single "Overnight Success," which hit the upper half of the R&B charts. A year later, she and her sisters veered away from the glossier pop of their recent releases and debuted a harder street edge with Serious Slammin', their final album for RCA Records. Immediately, fans and critics hailed it as the strongest of the sisters' four releases for RCA. People magazine, for one, proclaimed the album a "delight" and called the Pointers "the best R&B female group of the '80s."

But despite such praise, the Pointer Sisters felt it was time for a change. They'd spent the last 10 years working with Richard Perry, their contract with RCA had run its course, and a new decade was on the horizon. Starting fresh yet again, the sisters parted ways with Perry and signed with Motown Records. As a solo artist, June signed with Columbia Records, which released her second solo album, simply titled June Pointer, in the summer of 1989.

In 1990, the Pointers released their debut on Motown, Right Rhythm, which featured a mixture of hip-hop, street sounds and their trademark harmonies. It was the first time the sisters served as executive producers; they also contributed to the writing, something they hadn't done in several years. The album's percolating first single, "Friends Advice (Don't Take It)," hit the top 40 on the R&B charts. A second release, the ballad "After You," didn't make much impact on the charts, but a remix of "Insanity" by Steve "Silk" Hurley, took the club world by storm and peaked at #11 on Billboard's dance charts.

Nineteen ninety-three marked the Pointer Sisters 20th year in the recording industry, and they helped celebrate the anniversary with a new album, entitled Only Sisters Can Do That, on SBK Records. All three sisters wrote material for the album, including the title track, which the Pointers penned together. Other stand-outs on the album included "It Ain't a Man's World," which incorporated the poetry of Maya Angelou, and "I Want Fireworks," a gospel-tinged ballad that was propelled by Anita's soulful lead vocal. Once again, fans and critics alike sang the record's praises--Entertainment Weekly, for one, called Only Sisters "catchier than En Vogue or Janet Jackson" and proclaimed it "the catchiest Sisters set since 1984's hit-packed Break Out."

Over the next few years, Ruth, Anita and June
continued to charge on. In 1994, they teamed up with
Clint Black to record a cover of "Chain of Fools" for
MCA's Rhythm, Country & Blues, which was certified
platinum. That same year, a massive crowd swarmed to
Hollywood Boulevard to see the Pointers finally receive
a star on the Hollywood Walk of Fame, an event that
inspired town officials to proclaim it "Pointer Sisters Day"
in Hollywood. That same day, it was announced that the
group would once again don feather boas and platform
heels and begin a world-wide tour of the Fats Waller
musical "Ain't Misbehavin'. " They toured with the show
for 46 weeks and recorded a cast album that was hailed
by critics. The sisters went on to be honored on the Soul
of American Music Awards and were also inducted into
the Soul Train Hall of Fame. In 1996, they were one of
the legendary acts that performed at the closing
ceremony of the Olympics in Atlanta, and the group was
saluted with Fire--The Very Best of the Pointer Sisters, a
36-song anthology that chronicled the sisters' career,
from "Don't Try to Take the Fifth" all the way to the RCA
years.

Today, Ruth Pointer, along with her daughter and
granddaughter maintain a busy touring schedule and
perform all over the world. Best of all, Ruth and Anita
can look back on a career that has been filled with
endless applause, countless awards and legendary
performances. And though that career has now spanned
over 40 years, the excitement continues on! "We all like
showing off too much to stop," June told a reporter in

1997. "Honestly, all I've ever done in my life is entertain .
. . I feel like God has given us a gift, and it's our job to
share it with the world."

Anita Pointer, one of the Grammy grant winning Pointer Sisters whose series of hits included Programmed and I'm So Energized, has kicked the bucket matured 74. She was encircled by family at her Beverly Slopes home in California when she passed on New Year's Eve, her marketing specialist, Roger Neal, said.

In an explanation, her family said they were profoundly disheartened by the misfortune. "She was the one that kept us all nearby and together for such a long time," they said. "Her affection for our family will live on in every one of us. Paradise is a really cherishing, lovely spot with Anita there."

The Pointer Sisters bunch was at first two sisters, June and Bonnie, who proceeded as a pair in the last part of the 1960s. Anita, the second most seasoned, and Ruth, the most youthful, consequently joined and they delivered their presentation collection, The Pointer Sisters, with their most memorable hit single, Yes We Can, in 1973.

In 1975 their tune Fantasy, composed by Anita and Bonnie with Anita on lead vocals, won a Grammy for best country vocal execution. It prompted the Pointer Sisters turning into the primary dark female gathering to perform at the Fantastic Ole Opry in Nashville.

Bonnie left in 1978 and the gathering practically disbanded. However, they kept on and it was Anita, June and Ruth who then came to stratospheric business progress during the 1980s with top 10 hits that likewise included Hop (For My Adoration), Slow Hand, He's So Bashful and Fire, composed by Bruce Springsteen.

Their tune Neutron Dance turned out to be far superior when it was utilized in the film Beverly Slopes Cop to the opening and marvelously crash-filled pursuit succession.

In 1987 Anita delivered her most memorable independent collection, Love for What It Is, and the single Unexpected phenomenon.

Pointer resigned from acting in 2015. Ruth is currently the main enduring Pointer Sister, as June passed on in 2006 and Bonnie in 2020. Anita's girl, Jada, passed on in 2003, driving Anita to assume control over raising her granddaughter, Roxie McKain Pointer.

In their proclamation, the family said: "While we are profoundly disheartened by the deficiency of Anita, we are supported in realizing she is currently with her girl Jada and her sisters June and Bonnie and settled."

Many offered recognition via virtual entertainment. Katrina Leskanich, of Katrina and the Waves, was on a visit with Wham! furthermore, the Pointer Sisters in 1985. "Anita was so kind and liberal with her fellowship and direction to me. I gained some significant experience standing side stage consistently watching her astound and energize the group.

"While watching Wham!, she let me know something I will always remember. 'Everything revolves around energy.' Thank you for your energy and enthusiasm and the music that makes me and the world love you to such an extent.

Chapter two

Bunch Bio of pointers sisters

"The blood that Jesus shed for me way back on Calvary
The blood that invigorates me from one day to another
it won't ever lose His power"

It was around forty years prior when those words were sung in the Congregation of God in West Oakland, California. There, the Reverend Elton Pointer and his significant other Sarah both served over a little gathering while at the same time bringing up their six youngsters: two young men, Fritz and Aaron, and the four young ladies who gave voice to "The Blood"- - Ruth, Anita, Bonnie and June- - similar young ladies who might proceed to accomplish overall notoriety and secure a spot in popular music history.

The Pointer Sisters' dazzling achievement positively misrepresents such humble starting points, yet the people who know the genuine story of their childhood just wonder about their accomplishments even more. Since, regardless of the way that the sisters previously hit it huge with a melody called "Yes We Can," the well established strict convictions held by Elton and Sarah made "no" a prevalent word in the Pointer family. "No adornments, no cosmetics, no moving, no motion pictures, and positively no awesome music," Ruth told Quintessence magazine while reviewing her life as a

youngster in 1981. "Daddy needed to shield us from
what he called 'Satan's work,' and he endeavored to
ensure he did." And with six kids to raise, Elton and his
better half buckled down to get by - however as a rule,
they saw that as troublesome. Anita, truth be told, said
she got another dress just two times every year: when
on Easter, and once at Christmas. "We assumed we
were the least fortunate individuals on the planet," Ruth
told a questionnaire in 1980. "The vast majority of our
garments came from the Salvation Armed force, Father
Heavenly's secondhand shop and church scrounge
deals." "Circumstances were quite difficult," June
concurs. "All we truly needed to satisfy us was our
voices."

Adequately sure, the Pointers' skill for singing had
proactively become obvious. Truth be told, June says,
the sisters had been singing before they might walk- - a
delight that just developed as the young ladies did.
Some of the time, they'd impersonate the tunes they had
heard on TV - periodically, they were permitted to watch
an innocuous Western. Different times, they'd sing the
gospel numbers they'd heard in their folks' congregation.
However, most frequently, when they were securely
away from the meddlesome ears of Sarah and Elton,
they'd sing an alternate sort of music- - the caring they'd
heard on the radio in companions' and neighbors'
homes. Also, to go with it, they'd utilize the "instruments'
' they could find. "Our people would take off from the
house, and we'd get in the back room and beat a pie
container with spoons, making that cadence and sticking

together," June told a questionnaire in 1981. "At the point when they'd get back home, Granddad would agree, 'Better whip their butts- - they were in there popping their fingers and shaking their behinds, singing the blues! Horrible! Horrible!' And we'd get a whipping, as well - no doubt."

As the sisters developed, they carried their voices to the spot that gave them their most memorable proper preparation - and their most memorable crowd: their folks' congregation. There, they sang together in the congregation's ensemble - "The Blood " was one of their main tunes to perform. At last, youthful Ruth started coordinating the lesser ensemble, however in a little while, the sisters' advantage in music extended and demonstrated areas of strength for excessively their folks to corral. At some point, Ruth brought back her most memorable record buy, Elvis Presley's "All Stirred Up," and, shockingly, the sisters were really permitted to play it. "I think it even got into the house because in light of the fact that 'Crying in the Sanctuary' was on the opposite side, and Mother enjoyed that melody," Anita told a questionnaire in 1993. "That was one of the first non-gospel melodies that we were permitted to play."

Just out of secondary school, Ruth and Anita wedded and started bringing up kids, yet Bonnie had different plans. As Sarah told Midnight magazine in 1974, "(Bonnie) had consistently told me, 'Mother, I need something for myself; I need to be someone in this world.' " Persuaded that music was her purpose in life,

she enrolled June to join her in a singing team called
Pointers- - A Couple, and the two started acting in clubs
around the Straight region. In a little while, Anita quit her
place of employment at a legitimate office to join the
overlap, and the Pointer Sisters were formally
conceived.

Yet, the road to popularity ended up being a rough one:
as Sarah reviewed in a 1993 meeting, her little girls
headed out to Texas in 1969 to "track down their
fortune," however the excursion transformed into a
calamity. At the point when the young ladies were
abandoned in Houston, "they called and needed a way
home," Sarah reviews. "I said, I can't send for every one
of you, yet I'll send for June- - that is my child!' " In
retelling the disaster years after the fact, Anita giggled,
"That is the point at which we called David Rubinson."
Yet there was one trick: the sisters had never at any
point met Rubinson, one of the accomplices in Bill
Graham's record names - Bonnie had simply known
about him. Steadfast, she got the telephone and
snagged him. "I called him and said, 'You don't have any
acquaintance with us, and you've never heard us sing,
yet if it's not too much trouble, trust us and help!'"

Luckily, Rubinson consented to assist and sent the
sisters admission back to California, where he got them
work singing reinforcement on studio meetings by Taj
Mahal, Beauty Smooth, Boz Scaggs and others. At last,
Graham signed them to an administration contract, and
in 1971, Atlantic Records VP Jerry Wexler heard the

gathering backing Elvin Cleric at the Bourbon A Go in Los Angeles and offered them a record bargain.

Prior to entering the studio, the sisters chose to make their recording debut by singing a cappella, however as per Anita, Atlantic scoffed at the idea. "They said, " You can't sing stuff like that," she reviews. All things being equal, apprehensive chiefs chose to avoid any unnecessary risk, and had the gathering record two tunes with a conventional Honeycomb sound, one being "Don¹t Attempt To Take The Fifth" with June on lead vocal. In any case, when that record was delivered, it was met with a tepid gathering, and "the main spot it was heard was in our front rooms," Anita says.

In August 1971, Rubinson left Bill Graham's overlap and began his own creation organization, David Rubinson and Companions. The next year, when the Pointers' administration and Atlantic arrangements were up, they endorsed Rubinson, who vowed to deliver their presentation collection on his new Blue Thumb name. On occasion, Ruth had filled in for June and had been watching her more youthful sisters from the sidelines: "I saw them returning home - stumbling, honey, they were having a great time," she told Black magazine. "I said hi, look here, this is for me. That is the point at which I understood what I needed to do." So in December of 1972, Ruth quit her place of employment as a keypunch administrator and joined the gathering, and the sisters turned into a group of four.

As the Pointers started planning to record their
presentation collection, they settled on one firm choice:
record leaders be accursed, they'd sing the sort of music
they needed to sing, and that implied shunning the
sounds on Top 40 radio and recording a collection
included jazz, scat and bebop. Pushing at maximum
speed forward, they started composing jazz material for
the collection, however there was as yet one issue: the
gathering required execution dresses, yet focusing on
no additional money, architect ensembles were not
feasible. Searching for thoughts, the Pointers reviewed
how their folks had figured out how to dress six
youngsters on such a limited spending plan - and
simultaneously, they concocted a shrewd thought: by
and by, they'd raise a ruckus around town stores, and
sing.

Chapter three

Why Everyone In Music Should Read Ruth Pointer's Autobiography

30 years level-headed, the oldest of The Pointer Sisters has delivered a tell-all journal that contains significant examples about the music business, love, and life.

The Pointer Sisters got the web well before they got the web. They might be one of America's top rated young lady gatherings, with a vocation traversing fifty years and three Grammys to their name, however the senses that drove their prosperity share a great deal for all intents and purposes with the present culture-mining millennial mentality. During the '70s and '80s, when classification lines were defined along racial boundaries and policed by radio broadcasts and pundits the same, The Pointer Sisters had pop hits, electronic hits, jazz hits, and, surprisingly, a down home music hit — meanwhile being sorted by the business as a R&B bunch. Recalling that makes late discussions about "the new R&B" and "alt-R&B" — thoughts that eradicate R&B's imagination — feel considerably more obsolete than they previously did.

"Individuals continued to say, 'You must pick a class," Ruth Pointer let me know via telephone from her home beyond Boston mid one January morning. "Why? For what reason do you need to do that? It wasn't something we believed we needed to do." In spite of making progress with their imaginative, against perfectionist approach, they got an analysis for sounding "excessively white" — yet that didn't upset them. In 1975, the sisters — Ruth, Anita, Bonnie, and June — won their most memorable Grammy for their vocal presentation of "Fantasy," a bluegrass melody written by the gathering's most youthful two kin that Elvis Presley proceeded to cover in a television special. The prior year, they'd turn into the primary people of color to perform at down home music's congregation, Nashville's Stupendous Ole Opry, likely stirring up a lot of disarray for down home music fans who had no clue The Pointer Sisters were dark. Turning the tables with each record, they even made a tune that addresses the present cyborg style — 1984's "Programmed" that is as yet a staple in U.K. clubs and bars — and won a Grammy for it: I'm strolling blindfolded/Totally programmed/my frameworks are all down.

The tune's incomprehensibly low lead vocal has a place with Ruth, the oldest of the sisters. This month sees the arrival of her self-portrayal, Still So Energized — a reference to the gathering's most well known tune, the pop-rock hit "So Energized" — which lifts the top on what stratospheric notoriety in that generally famous of times was truly similar to. It's a grasping read, not only for the music business experiences and the sisters' glitzy takes advantage of yet for the explicitness with which Ruth portrays the chronic drug use that nearly took her life, and destroyed those of her most treasured.

Bonnie wound up leaving the gathering in 1978 and has had a long and irrefutably factual fight with her own dependence, as did most youthful sister June, who passed on from disease in 2006. Nowadays, Ruth — who is presently 30 years sober — and Anita keep on proceeding as The Pointer Sisters with Ruth's girl or granddaughter alternating to go along with them in front of an audience.

Via telephone, Ruth Pointer is similarly however immediate as she seems to be on paper, with none of the subject-changing cushion that frequently litters the discourse of the present stars. There is no faltering in her profound, rich voice while wrestling with what most would consider troublesome or difficult subjects. She's survived a great deal however nothing's dulled her want life or her adoration for music. There's a piece in the book that maybe best outlines her soul: as a little kid experiencing childhood in a severe and strict family, Ruth would frequently go dependent upon her cohorts and welcome herself over to their home for supper. "Thinking back," she states, "I was interested in the way that others lived and needed to taste it for myself.

The Pointer Sisters had hits in essentially every sort. There's something very "web" about that methodology in that you're connecting with everything and anything since you can. What energized that imaginative interest in every one of you?

RUTH POINTER: I think we just didn't have any desire to be categorized into one class. We grew up cherishing a wide range of music from old style to country, R&B and gospel. We adored everything. Individuals continued to say, "You must pick a class!" Why? For what reason do you need to do that? It wasn't something we believed we needed to do.

It's so weird today when I stand by listening to the radio and they have what I generally knew as R&B recorded as jazz or simple tuning in. Truly? Presently R&B is hip-jump.

There weren't numerous different demonstrations moving between sorts as you did. Other than having an interest in music, what was pushing that want not to be categorized?

It appeared to be that every one of the greater awards were going into the white classifications. The R&B craftsmen weren't winning Grammys. That is the reason when we won the Grammy for the bluegrass melody "Fantasy," we were in shock. They let us know when we were out and about; we weren't even at the service.

I likewise think it has to do with the tone of a vocalist's style that they need to place you in a classification. We've never had that regular kind of R&B dark sound during our manners of speaking since we didn't grow up singing in a congregation. We heard gospel on the radio.

We got reprimanded a great deal for "sounding white." When we did the "Fantasy" melody, individuals in Nashville didn't actually realize we were dark.

One of the minutes in the book that consumes into your mind is when, at a private all-nighter following your presentation in Nashville in 1975, you and your sisters were taken around the rear of the house and left to sit in the kitchen in light of the fact that the individual who addressed the entryway thought you were employed assistance. Do you feel like the music business has gotten any less bigoted than it was then? Have you seen it change throughout the long term?

I have seen it change because of current innovation like virtual entertainment. Some time ago, you were helpless before the radio or turned tables. You didn't have the arrival that these children do today. The children in the white areas presently can tune into anything that music they need to experience and they like it.

Once upon a time, it was exceptionally isolated. A white radio broadcast wouldn't play Little Richard or Hurl Berry. That is the reason the progress of Pat Boone and Elvis went along. They could record a melody that Little Richard or Throw Berry composed and it would turn into a hit when nobody would have heard it before from the first creator. It's different these days. My children turn me onto stuff I have never heard.

It was extremist that you recorded anything you desired to record.

We were fortunate that we had a maker and chief David Rubinson. He was extremely open imaginatively for us to do what we felt like we needed to do. He was certainly not an unbending individual and truly cherished being around us and our innovative capacities. We had loads of tomfoolery.

Do you suppose the music business has changed in its treatment of ladies?

That is an extreme inquiry for me to respond to on the grounds that I actually see a ton of double-dealing with ladies in the business. Recordings are simply so physically realistic rather than when a lady could remain in a sequined outfit before a receiver and sing her butt off. Presently she's have to really show her butt or purchase another butt to draw in the consideration. That is genuine.

Is there anything you think any young lady beginning in the music business ought to be aware or endeavor to follow?

We were performing with the Enticements and they pulled us to the side and said, "Tune in, you all need to truly focus on your business." I see these youngsters are substantially more forceful about that than we were. I feel that has a ton to do with why they're turning out to be so monetarily effective nowadays, more than we were. They're dealing with their own business and I'm genuinely glad for them for doing that. Focus on those numbers and don't take no for a response. I respect pretty much every one of the ladies, regardless of what sort of butts they have.

"We were performing with the Enticements and they pulled us to the side and said, 'Tune in, you folks need to truly focus on your business.' I see these youngsters are considerably more forceful about that than we were. They're taking care of their own business and I'm truly pleased with them for doing that." — Ruth Pointer
We live during a time of truly politicized performers. We frequently hope to start to stand up on issues. Is there anything you wish you had been more blunt on at that point?

I regret absolutely nothing about the manner in which things have shown up for us. We got a supernatural occurrence that I hadn't anticipated. I was somewhat moving alongside the bazaar. I want to have been more clear and made that excursion without the utilization of substances, yet I couldn't say whether it would have been unique. Perhaps that was only my way to have the option to have this story and ideally help another person who's going down that street. That is my motivation for the book in any case, to give individuals trust and to comprehend that they don't need to remain in that life.

What compelled you to share such a great amount in your self-portrayal, Still So Energized?

I surmise inside the most recent thirty years, which has been the greatest piece of my recuperation from medications and liquor, there were simply things occurring in my life as I aged that I felt were the beauty of the universe or God or some higher power here and there that was safeguarding me and saving me here for reasons unknown. It made me need to impart my encounters and offer to individuals not to surrender. The expectation of proceeding to carry on with a positive life can be so motivating and fulfilling. To simply continue getting up and placing slowly but surely, these truly extraordinary things began to occur in my life.

It could have all the earmarks of being second to other people, yet the way that I could get past the disorder of meningitis, and that I could traverse a blood coagulation in my lung, and overcome a couple of operations was faltering to me. I saw my mates kicking the bucket around me for things that I accepted weren't anyway serious as what I appeared to be going through and I was very much like, "Amazing. Somebody is looking after me."

You must give yourself some credit, as well.

Indeed, that is the thing. I turned my life around thus ordinarily I hear today what you said, and my sibling expresses that to me as well. "You need to give yourself some credit."

I changed essentially everything in my life when I chose to surrender those substances that I believed were killing me. I moved into an area where individuals that I used to realize that enjoyed that way of life couldn't get to me, I became resolved about not needing those things around me so much that it irritated individuals I truly cherished. I basically isolated myself from even some relatives. I was separated from everyone else a ton, however it was OK since I was level-headed. I was getting perfect, clear, and solid.

When you were moving out of those most reduced lows, what were the pragmatic everyday things that assisted you with remaining on track?

I nodded off on time around evening time, which was something uncommon that I hadn't done in numerous years. I was inclined to remain up the entire evening and at times keep awake for a few days enjoying medications and liquor. I didn't give a great deal of thought to my well-being like that. I got up early enough to have straightforward things like a morning meal.

Something that began happening to me when I surrendered the substances is that I began gobbling up food, which is something I began utilizing these substances to keep away from. It was my weight control and diet, and I thought it was alright. At the point when I began to eat once more, that frightened me. I had attempted to quit utilizing it a few times, however when I began eating once more, I thought, "I can't do this." I detested being fat and I didn't need that self-perception of myself.

I began to search out various ways of controlling my eating and I found a 12-step program that assisted me with pulling some coordinated programs for food. The more I remained in that program, the more I found out about food compulsion and it captivated me. I used to set my clock so I could awaken, have my morning meal, and afterward have a specific measure of hours among breakfast and lunch, so it would be undeniably offset to five to six hours each. Then, I could nod off at a specific time.

I actually did that today. It's making another propensity that I think made me better and I appreciate it. I truly value its discipline. I utilize a scale to gauge every one of my dinners. My two most youthful children, that is the main way they know me. They're 22 now, and they even have concerns. My little girl will sporadically go, "Mother, is this a decent dinner?" And my child will request that I fix him a plate of mixed greens. It motivates and comes off on individuals around me, which is definitely not something terrible.

You referenced utilizing substances to hold your weight down in the early long stretches of being in the Pointer

Sisters. Was this something far reaching in the business — was it supported?

I think it was energized. One of my fondest recollections was the absolute first Saturday Night Live program that included Desi Arnaz who came on the set with a barrel of cocaine and white powder by and large around his face and said, "This is my eating regimen!" Many individuals recall that scene and we believe it's diverting. In any case, during the '70s and '80s, ladies as well as both male and females involved cocaine as an eating routine enhancement. It was fun, it was not difficult to get, and you didn't have a craving when you utilized it. Nobody was discussing the drawback of it by any means by then. Nobody was biting the dust, nobody was saying you'll be dependent. Truly, Richard Pryor pokes an incredible fun at what he did when he was alive doing his phenomenal: "Cocaine Isn't habit-forming; I've been involving it for quite some time!"

"I changed essentially everything in my life when I chose to surrender those substances that I believed were killing me. I was distant from everyone else a ton, yet it was OK since I was level-headed. I was getting perfect, clear, and sound." — Ruth Pointer
Richard Pryor and Muhammad Ali are among the stars that spring up in the book — it portrays VIP life during the '70s and '80s. What was the best recommendation an individual illuminator gave you during those times?

Wow...I can't actually recollect a ton of that time sadly [laughs]. Individuals that we worked with were so proficient. I'm thinking about the incomparable Tune Burnett, who is still with us, expressing gratitude toward God. We worked with her for a really long time. She just took to us like we were her daughters and was continually having us on her show. We even went out and about with her. We gained one of the most incredible illustrations from her: you set up a closet for your street show, and that is the idea of the show consistently. We had never heard that.

At the point when we came into the business, we were wearing one of a kind garments that were exceptionally delicate. We assumed we should be runway models and wear something else consistently. We were going through those garments like water. It was becoming very pricey. Furthermore, the more reputation we were getting, the more costly those rare garments began to be. So when we met Hymn Burnett, she let us know this is the closet for the visit and this is the thing we'll wear consistently. That was quite possibly the best example we learned.

Beyond the material things and honors, what does music give you personally?

Music resembles the air I relax in. I love it to such an extent. It could change my disposition for the afternoon; it can change my mentality briefly. I had a photograph taken a day or two ago and we were playing clear music the entire day. Me and the young ladies were discussing this exceptionally subject of what music means for us. I love paying attention to music in my vehicle since it seems like I'm sitting in the speaker. Assuming my main tune comes on and I'm maneuvering into the carport, I can't escape the vehicle. It's practically similar to I'm in a climax, as don't move, don't move!

I'm enamored with Chris Earthy colored voice, however terrible as he seems to be. I love Kanye West, I love Rihanna! I love Drake and The Weeknd.

"Assuming my main tune comes on and I'm maneuvering into the carport, I can't escape the vehicle. It's practically similar to I'm in a climax, as 'don't move, don't move!'" — Ruth Pointer
You hint in the book under one of the photographs that there may be new music from you later on. Is that something we can anticipate?

That would be loads of good times for me, there's actually individuals calling me saying that they're pausing. Be that as it may, I'm not up on the new recording systems and I realize things have changed a great deal. Individuals are paying for their own items, which I'm not used to doing.

At the point when you were beginning, the names resembled divine beings as it were and they controlled everything. Presently, the most intriguing individuals going along are doing everything without a mark.

That is what I was referring to before! That is the reason they're so monetarily fruitful; they don't owe anyone anything, which I love. I would rather not owe anyone anything. I'm attempting to teach myself so I can approach getting it done and not have any terrible sentiments about a misfortune or have somebody keeping down my item for a moronic explanation.

We did delightful accounts of a couple Christmas tunes a couple of years prior with my sister and girl. But since of some sort of political stuff between individuals who were funding the undertaking, it was never under any circumstance delivered. I couldn't start to envision the number of superb, creative things we don't get to hear on account of wildness like that. Each opportunity Christmas goes along I ponder that — God, those tunes should be on the radio!

I couldn't want anything more than to follow through with something, I have thoughts. I simply have to get with the perfect individuals to do it so it won't be a misfortune for me.

Close to the furthest limit of the book, you say you keep Obama and his family in your requests. Will you be loaning your help to any other individual?

I'm truly torn. What's more, observing this multitude of insane legislators battle with one another, I'm similar to wow...I have barely any insight into any of you folks! I love the Obama family and I figure they did all that could be expected with what they had before them, what they needed to work with. I think they'll be feeling significantly better to get the damnation out of there. I believe they're delightful individuals and I keep them in my requests since I accept they need that; it's a difficult situation.

chapter four

BONNIE POINTER

our life. I as of now miss her, and I will see her again one day." No reason was given.

The Pointer Sisters developed from The Pointers - A Couple, a San Francisco-based bunch Bonnie framed in 1969 with her more youthful sister, June. The team performed R&B covers in Oakland clubs and was essential for the Northern California State Youth Ensemble. Anita Pointer saw her sisters singing with the ensemble at the Fillmore West and quickly quit her legitimate secretary task to sing with them.

The Pointers grew up singing in the ensemble at their dad's Oakland church, and had surreptitious meetings paying attention to mainstream radio when their folks weren't home: Nina Simone, Elvis Presley, Sam Cooke, Etta James. Afterward, the kin worked enthusiastically on their music — practicing, composing and orchestrating vocals, and writing unique melodies — and absorbing the progressive governmental issues, culture and music stirring late-'60s San Francisco.

As a triplet, they diverted their varied melodic preferences and stage insight into gigs singing reinforcement for Effortlessness Smooth, Sylvester, Boz Scaggs and Elvin Minister. Bonnie — an expressive, light entertainer who easily embraced components of soul, pop and jazz — particularly inclined toward such melodic flexibility. "I'm the sort of individual who likes to do brave, new things - it must be quite difficult for me to proceed, on the grounds that I could do without to be stuck into only a certain something," she told Blues and Soul in 1979.

That disposition likewise summed up The Pointer Sisters' initial work, which opposed the arrangement. An early arrangement with Atlantic Records went south after the name attempted to push them toward direct R&B. In Fantasy: The Pointer Sisters' Family Story, Anita Pointer reviewed that Bonnie was particularly determined that the gathering needed to sound diverse: "We've decided.We need to sing everything."

When sister Ruth joined the gathering and they found a home on the free name Blue Thumb, the Sisters' fortunes got to the next level. Their self-named debut LP, from 1973, opened with their most memorable hit — a swaggering front of Allen Toussaint's "Yes We Can" — and finished similarly as considerably, with a searing gospel-blues rendition of "Wang Darn." In the middle between, the Pointers addressed jazz, swing and Broadway.

"We must make this land/a preferred land/over the one in which we live," the Sisters sing in this Spirit Train execution from 1973.

The next year's ``That is By the drove'' included the delicate national anthem "Fantasy," which Bonnie and Anita co-composed. The melody moved over to the pop diagrams, won Best Country Vocal Execution by a Pair or Gathering at the Grammys, and was subsequently cut by Elvis Presley. Bonnie likewise co-composed that collection's blues-inclining "Unsteady Level Blues" with her sisters and followed that up with a credit on 1975's serene, steamy funk kiss-off "How Long (Betcha' Got a Chick as an afterthought)," one more hit.

Bonnie Pointer left the gathering in 1977, leaving a performance profession with two self-named collections. She found her greatest triumphs on the dance graphs, stirring things up around town 10 with fronts of Motown hits "I Can't Help Myself (Sugar Pie, Sweet bunch)" and "Paradise Probably Sent You." The last option was her greatest performance hit: In addition to the fact that she cut a more conventional rendition that highlighted a coda of her scat singing, however she likewise created a life-changing, extravagant disco take after she heard the Town Public's "Y.M.C.A."

"That gave me the plan to sing it like that," she said in 2013. "That is where we got the musicality and the beat. So I considered Berry Gordy and let him know that is what we needed to do. I didn't realize I planned to scat. That was off the cuff. I just did it at the time out of motivation."

In this freewheeling jazz number, the Sisters match the frantic speed of the piano and musicality segment, giving the presentation a winking jubilance.

The fifth offspring of the Reverend Elton Pointer and his better half, Sarah, Bonnie was conceived by Patricia Eva Pointer in Oakland in 1950. In Fantasy: The Pointer Sisters' Family Story, Anita Pointer said that the moniker Bonnie came from sitters seeing that the little kid was charming as a rabbit. In a surprising turn, Bonnie herself decided to alter the affectionate nickname, renaming herself Bonnie. "I like naming myself, such as making myself," she said in the book. "I'm the only one in the family with an epithet."

That kind of iconoclasm would be a sign of Bonnie's life and profession. She was a skilled visual craftsman and imaginative essayist as well as being a capable performer; Anita Pointer depicted her as "the visionary" of the family in Fantasy: The Pointer Sisters' Family Story, while long-term Pointer Sisters maker David Rubinson included the very book that Bonnie was "totally defiant. She is the soul of decisiveness and fearlessness. She has an unbelievably high energy and extraordinary approach to everyday life."

Pointer delivered another independent collection, 1984's In the event that the Value Is Correct, however to a great extent moved back from recording, save for 2011 Resembles a Picasso. She additionally incidentally rejoined with her sisters to perform. In late 2019, a fan caught Bonnie and Anita Pointer singing an off the cuff form of "Fire" at a Las Vegas bar — outlining their getting through vocal bond, however her outsized character.

"Bonnie's constantly had a specific following," Ruth Pointer said in 2009. "She was the spunkiest of all; she was the most brief of all. We would all be at the lodging sleeping and Bonnie would be out in the road, celebrating with the fans. They adored them, Bonnie, honey!"